MARVELS OF THE INVISIBLE

MARVELS *of the* INVISIBLE

Jenny Molberg

TUPELO PRESS
NORTH ADAMS, MASSACHUSETTS

Library of Congress Cataloging-in-Publication Data

Names: Molberg, Jenny, 1985- author.
Title: Marvels of the invisible / Jenny Molberg.
Other titles: Tupelo Press First / Second Book Award (Series)
Description: First paperback edition. | North Adams, Massachusetts : Tupelo
  Press, [2017] | Series: The Tupelo Press First / Second Book Award : The
  Berkshire Prize | Includes bibliographical references.
Identifiers: LCCN 2016053264 | ISBN 9781936797929 (pbk. original : alk. paper)
Classification: LCC PS3613.O445 A6 2017 | DDC 811/.6-dc23

Cover and text designed and composed in Avant Garde Gothic and Bodoni Antiqua
by Bill Kuch

First paperback edition: January 2017.

Lyrics from "Always on My Mind" on page 37 were written by Johnny
Christopher, Mark James, and Wane Carson and first recorded in 1972.

Lyrics from "Dark Was the Night" on page 60 were written and recorded by
Blind Willie Johnson in 1927.

Tupelo Press
P.O. Box 1767, North Adams, Massachusetts 01247
Telephone: (413) 664-9611 / editor@tupelopress.org / www.tupelopress.org

Tupelo Press is an award-winning independent literary press that publishes fine
fiction, nonfiction, and poetry in books that are a joy to hold as well as read.
Tupelo Press is a registered 501(c)(3) nonprofit organization, and we rely on public
support to carry out our mission of publishing extraordinary work that may be
outside the realm of the large commercial publishers. Financial donations are
welcome and are tax deductible.

For the women of my heart:
Susu, Mom, and Jamey

CONTENTS

∞

MARVELS OF THE INVISIBLE

ECHOLOCATION

I think of you, my lost girl, when the wing
of a tailfin rises beside the boat, dripping
in salted robes. This movement, like song,
pulls me under, where murk reveals
the obscurities of loss. The language
is epic, invisible, submarine. A child
hears her home in clefs of water, in whale song:
unfathomable, plosive, drummed, the loudest blues
on earth. A thousand feet down, more join in the refrain.
Another endangered syntax descends.

◊ ◊ ◊
◊

Nothing on the sonogram for weeks.
The nurse's dull hand like a river stone
on my belly; the doctor's wintry eyes
scolded me, I thought. Oh, secret grief.
Are we not all sick with our own scolding?
When they found your heartbeat
I thought, *This could be a girl.* Just as quick,
you were gone. The question, the what-if:
always regret. But that is too simple.
To regret is to be too late.
To regret is to refuse to swim further down.

◊ ◊ ◊
◊

On the operating table, I thought of Jonah:
three days, three nights he prophesied
in the sunken body's cave, his mean bed
the boggy, pagan tongue of a monstrous fish.
The squelched prayer, *When my life was ebbing*
away, I remembered you–then mercy,
the sonorous brute relieved of his god-
fearing freight. Jonah, spat out on the beach,
reborn in his fear, the heart of the sea a God-stone
in his gut. But the whale was the merciful one,
holding a dove on its tongue. Don't you see?
You pulled me from my mind's shadowed corners,
near drowned in the cage I'd made of my bones.

◊ ◊ ◊
◊

You were the bird inside my veins' blue trees.
That night, I woke; I remembered you—
a small heartbeat inside me gone still.
I try to convince myself of an afterlife:
when a whale dies, it lives a second time.
It must drop to great depths, then an ecosystem
is born of its body. The sleeper sharks will tear
soft tissue from the corpse, its skeleton
colonized by a million worms. A root-like structure
grows into the bone and all the little animals feed.
No one is sated. No one regrets.

◊ ◊
◊
◊ ◊

The dream again: a beach strewn with humpback calves.
Each spews its white jet into catacombs of air.
I press my whole body's strength against them
to no avail. The bodies are black dunes
on the mute white sand. I give up, walk the road
of corpses, and come to it, the puzzle:
the clean jaw of a female cow.
I measure the slow lines. Each baleen plate
a glassy divot. When my work is done,
I hear singing. The whales, fins like wings,
flood the atmosphere as clouds. The heaviest,
the lightest things. My heart is full of them.

◊ ◊ ◊
◊

I was prey in the hot slick belly of the sea.
I wanted to die of anger. I wanted
to watch all things burn. A tamarisk sprang up
beside me, and I thought it was God.
A worm ate the green plant and I thought, *God,*
devour me. But the worm was full
of the saltcedar leaves. The earth refused
to wake, to weep. So I walked the tide's edge
to hear the waves' hushed dirge.
The muted tongues of the dead whisper,
God is covetous. He will not tolerate your sorrow.
I lose what I love and stay alive. I try.

◊ ◊ ◊
◊

I walk the shallow water for what emerges
in its absence. And yours. Deep down,
whale song so loud: if not for ocean water,
the human ear would burst.
The sun harpoons the late day sky.
Beneath my feet, a million shards
of rock and shell, things that once lived.
And deeper, the call of one animal to another.
Now and again, you breach the heart's surface:
this is your sounding; this is your wake.

∞

MARVELS OF THE INVISIBLE

With your new Microset Model I, you will discover marvels
of the invisible.

—Instruction manual, 1950s

The night I find my father's toy microscope
in the hospital-cold of the empty house,
I dream of him, a boy in 1964. He crosses the yard,
kneels beneath the sprawling live oak,
and fills his specimen jar with fire ants.
His father, in the garage, sings softly in German,
mounting the head of a deer shot
that winter; its antlers blossom like capillaries.
My father is six years old. The light
spills in as he bends over the microscope
and folds a single ant onto a plastic slide. The body,
almost sickening in its translucence,
curls into itself; the bright red thorax, close up,
is butterscotch. Pressed beneath the plastic,
the antennae shiver and are still.

Half a century later, my mother's breasts
are removed. In the waiting room, my father
takes a pen from his white coat pocket,
and clicks open, and clicks closed.
When someone in the family asks
a question, he takes a walk. I go with him,
and we wind through orange-tiled hallways.
He shows me the room full of microscopes.
I imagine his eye, how it descends
like a dark blue planet,
and his breath as it clouds the lens.
He shows me the refrigerator

where they keep the malignant tissue.
He shows me the microtomes,
the biopsy needles, the organ baths.

In the recovery room, we listen
as my mother's new systems of blood vessels
shush through a speaker in the room.
My father comes in quietly,
places a white orchid beside her bed.
The large white blossoms are hands
cupping the empty air. Suspended there
is everything that came before this:
the day my parents met,
the wedding, each of the three children
so different from the others. His hands
that know, like breathing, every inch of her.
He matches his breath with hers,
as they do each night
in the slow river of a breathing house,
and beneath her skin, her blood blossoms.

MIRROR

The little girl spoons
the peas into the milk.
(How is it that those hands are mine?)
My mother's long hands,
reaching to pull the plates away.
My father's voice from under a door,
the balcony impatiens
that wither, fall, pucker, bloom,
today's sun that flirts,
the bee as it curves its abdomen over
a weed flower, the dog as it sniffs at the bee,
the dog in midair, the bee in its teeth,
the stinger's depression on tongue,
the flinch, the paw, the cower.

Hold a mirror up to clouds: you'll see.
The way our lives pass as storms.
The way I am young and old at once.
The way, when we remember,
we take out the memory, change it
before it returns to the cagy coves of the brain.
Seaweed in current as it wafts and sways,
knowing nothing of itself,
or the sea, or the moon as it pulls the sea,
or the fish that rubs with silvery scales,
like a cat would, against it.
I am all of this, and none.
By this, I mean God.

CHRYSALIS

I want to see, somewhere,
the hot, cocooned unfolding
of metamorphosis. The caterpillars
are flown in from El Salvador
or New Guinea, and inside
the dewed glass, shadows
of men in white coats cloak
the tic of emergent wings—
What of the future do you hold
inside yourself? See: if you take a scalpel
and puncture the chrysalis,
it will explode—yellow goo
of cells, burst cells, amino acids,
proteins, here a bit of gut,
here a bit of brain.

A thing builds a shell around itself,
dissolves, becomes another thing.
The way, when you are wrecked
with love, you take only what you need,
you, liquid version of yourself,
all heart cells and skin cells—
here a trough of heart,
here, gutter of liver, channel
of hearing or touch. What remains,
as with the caterpillar, is memory.
See, we melt entirely.

I have been a child, a lake, a glacier,
glacial pool, woman, river of woman,
another woman, an older one.

The oldest scientist asks, If we are all
creatures of transformation,
if we are never quite the same,
what are we
when we arrive at the moment of death?
It is easier to think in death
that I am me, but dying. See: 1668.
The Dutch naturalist Jan Swammerdam
dissects a caterpillar for Cosimo de Medici.
And though we now think
everything ends,
turns to soup, to river, to ash
and what's passed is past, he unfolds
the white sides of the insect and reveals
two wing-buds, tucked
tight inside the skin.

Now, as I watch the knife
pierce the chrysalis,
a river of cells swelling through
and out, I remember
what my father once said,
that what you see is only a fraction
of what you can believe,
and against the edge of the chrysalis,
embryonic half-wings twitch
without a body, waiting
for their slow decay, and then
for the next body
that opens itself
to the risk of flight.

NOCTURNE FOR THE ELEPHANT

In the upper menagerie at Exeter Change,
where walls are striped with iron cages,
a musician sits down at his piano forte
to play a nocturne for the animals.

To him, the audience is familiar, each
a different beast, and each in its prison.
Adagio, he plays, and when
his hands spill down the scale,

the Indian elephant tilts the broad leaves
of its ears forward; tusks blunder against bars
as ivory keys prod wooden hammers,
felt-covered, like the animal's ancient tread

on desert soil. The song is a downpour
and the elephant begins to pace. The pianist drops
to the low B-flat and, in the base of its throat,
the elephant echoes the tone—dirge for a time

when, head bowed, he plodded
into a pond, tube of his trunk sloped
to lift milky water to his mouth,
roping the trunk to drench

the ashen body, each wet-darkened foot
lifting, stirring, a vibrato of water
emitting, from the body, watery rings
which enclosed him, then disappeared.

HOUSE OF MAKING

Why have we stopped building shrines?
The human body in grief is a shrine.
No, the human body is made almost entirely of water.
The grieving body is limestone and sandstone and onyx.
When he died, I woke and knew. I had not seen him in years.
I searched online. The first result: his eulogy.
The body in love is made entirely of water.
I spent hours watching the radar, waiting
for the pain to curl down as a wave.
The body in death is soil and dust and flame.
What was I waiting for? An answer? An explanation?
When we lose someone young, we want something to build.
The body in grief is mortar and brick and sweat.
When the shrine is built and the buildings are empty,
  we long for another body.
The body in desire is vein and gall and pen and paper.
You want to know why he left the earth.
I want to know why I should stay.
A physicist has killed a yeast cell, amplified its sounds. Listen.
Many hands clapping. Cicadas. The sound of wings.
The sound of one cell dying and the earth's answering.
The music of one death. All the world continuing.
Yes, the sound of the body in prayer is made entirely of water.
Yes, it is made of yes, yes, yes, yes, yes.

NECROSIS

for my father

You, microscope, are a hungry priest. I wanted
to confess to you: the nursing home, the fear
of travel, the land, sold long ago.
But you were too busy,
combing the pantry of diagnoses.
Molar pregnancy: bloody grapes, endometriotic
sac: chocolate cyst. A slice of grapefruit leiomyoma.
Only God's fingers could become so small.
Your lenses are the wooden crosshatch
of a confessional, eyes darting in the gaps.
I could see Him in a young girl's
bone marrow. Her cells swelled,
vacuolized: ribosomes, cytoplasm, leaking
like spilled jelly. I draw the lens to a focus.
You can never know repentance.

SUPERFICIAL HEART

It's monstrous already, the human heart, so think
of the child born with her heart outside her body.
It pulses in a membrane sac like a frog's
translucent throat—oversized, two-chambered,
auricle, ventricle. The fist-beat of it, her mother thinks,
must be contained. And so with two pillows, she dams
the heart—the heart, inside the crib, a tremor
in water, impossible to hold or protect. Days later, death.

    If only she'd lived.
With sentinel hands placed over the heart, her mother
would wade with her into the pond, or let her
whisk the eggs for breakfast, pushed back
from the stove; later, when she was older, short walks
on the moor, a book before bed. And at night,
as the child rocked between two pillows, kindling
caught in tide, her heart would burst, again and again.

THE DREAM, THE SLEEPING GYPSY

In what would be his last work,
Henri Rousseau painted a moon
in place of the sun, passive

as a dying woman. With his brush
he lit the girl's breasts,
two bright pomelos, the orbed

voyeuristic eyes of the lioness.
My mother's skin is artless,
her hands deft. She turns each page,

whispering the names. Seeing
in Rousseau not shadowless
brushwork, not a child's misconception

of the world as flat, but layers
over layers, his hand patient
as the acacia that rings its own grain

while the years pass, its wide taproot
drawing up from the earth
a strange, unutterable music.

I want to say my mother loves
the gourd-like lute as the thing
that most reflects the moon,

for it moves the eye from depth
to surface as if they were
the same. The few incisions

of light in the desert sky
strike the woman's long
sleeping hair, the lion beside her.

The moon's face
a cold white god. This
is the metastasizing beauty

of my mother. My mother the gypsy.
I, the pinpricked sky.
The lion her cancer.

PHOSPHENE

There is a way to see the other world.
My father quarters the red potatoes,
strips the husks from the corn
like little dresses, extracting
the shrimp from their shells
while I, on my back
in the sun, press my finger
against my eye because when I do
globes appear over and over.
Some are red; some are long-dead stars.
When a slit of sunlight
rushes in, I shut tightly the doors,
and close my ears to stop
the paddle of waves or somewhere
a gull, wrenching open a clam, the squeak
of a crab's machine-like legs. And after
the shrimp shells, my father plucks the legs
in fingerfulls. He pushes my mother
gently with the blunt
of his hand on the small
of her back from the kitchen.
I orbit the low red sun, keep
pressing and pressing. My father
stirs each ingredient into the pot
by a timer. By now, I know
his knife is running along their backs.
Or he is washing the veins down the sink. Or
look, look at the sun on the bay. It's in flames.

∞

POMEGRANATE

Before I crack open the fruit,
the seeds swell in their white caves, clatter
and hum—red voices muffled by pulp.
A song of berries. The fruit swings on a branch
and the seeds clink together and ring out, one
of the seven fruits of Israel.

613 berries—distended arils—
the Torah's 613 commandments.

Or, I am Persephone and for four months I will
pull apart the flesh, and it will be winter.
Winter is the pomegranate's season.
My hands are stained. I pick the seeds apart.
The only sound is a soft click: one last note
as they fall. With each tiny death, I am fed.

OUR LADY OF THE RIO GRANDE

for my sister

I let you walk ahead:
blued silhouette, little
sister, luz de día in desert,
dazzling, dressed in what you've yet
to live. Bulbs buzz
in the barracks. Standing before
incendiary hallways,
we are parallel in panels
of electrified glass, rarefied neon:
mock mirage in this,
the West Texas we knew, noble
gas, glow lamp, plasma, you
on one side of the light and I
on the other. This is how
we see ourselves,
swelling out like hours.
Us, Texas, the hills
bulbous as fractured skulls
dusted and surging, sanded smooth—
you, stepping back from the light,
I, stepping towards, backlit by blue.
You, humming violent, violet,
now yellowed, not yellow of aging
but yellow of new light or
yellow of our aging together. You,
little echo of me; me, looking on
now green, now blue, now violet, now pink.
Little sister of light and dark.

Little wasteland beacon.
Little saint of glowing hope, scintillating
in tumbleweed wind.
What lies ahead of you. What lies
behind me, pulsing fluorescent
in the red canyon between us.

ATROPOS

for my Opa

In March, the hill country is an opus
of golden-cheeked warblers, the immutable
turn of constellations. When flocks

of clouds pass over, so do the birds,
pulled by earth's magnet, or what lies below—
a tribe of dreams, sleep gods.

Dusk in my grandfather's house: sharp
cedar smell, night dancing along window glass
like branches or fingers. Memory,

that dusky goddess, sleeps with no one.
And when Opa wakes, the Alzheimer's
wave of unfamiliar voices is wind

drowned in clouds, and now his body, too,
gale in the tallest juniper, a rustle
of warbler wings, Indian paintbrush

blistering the lawn. The fates weigh out
good and evil in some future version of me.
When she is born, stars

will burst from my chest, will burrow in sky.
Please, little someone, little not-yet-born:
for us, remember.

BATHSHEBA AS POET

Her lamp is never extinguished at night.
                                    —Proverbs 31:18

Cooing at the mikvah: a silver rock dove
behind my wicker screen. A demon come
to curse my bath—another childless month.

Rustle of feathers. I turn back to look.
The screen, split open as a lanced melon.
The speared bird. David, at the opening.

I grow rounder every day; I write
my husband a new woman. I write his end
and my child's beginning. Pen her fingers'

whorls, press the soft clay of her cartilage
to bone. Smooth the wrinkled paper
of her skin, and with a flourish, the dark wisps

around her eyes begin to follow light.
Because I do not deserve this joy,
with God's help, I also write my child's death.

I'm a second wife, the author of false verse.
I have broken my name's oath. I have written woman
as a myth, an omnipotent ghost.

CHRISTENING

My mother is writing *blue/brown* under "eye color."
I am in an incubator, jaundiced. She is turning
names over in her head. They had wanted
to name me Melissa, like the Cretan,
or my father's sister. But Mom sees
that I do not have the blue eyes of my father.
She recognizes her own dark
flash. And so she chooses a name
she knows well. When she utters it
for the first time, I do not hear. My eyes are covered
with a sterile blindfold and a blue light
breaks up the bilirubin in my liver like glass.
Later, the blue eye slowly turns until
indistinguishably umber, like its match.

I AM NOT THINE, BUT THEE

after Katherine Philips

A child is born in Winslow, Arkansas.
He will one day be the man

who tells me I am nothing, the man
I want to forgive, but can't.

Bald infant pitch, echo of cedar and ash.
Grandfathers, the undulant hum

of rocking chairs. Fathers,
breaking sticks in halves and fourths.

It never begins or ends, this,
what we learn from men,

what violence, what mercy.
The child is born to a midwife.

The midwife will be the woman
who one day tells me, Leave him.

He is just like his father.
She is sometimes me.

She is also the bite of the woods
and the bend of the foothill,

a warm egg beneath a hen,
the cucumbers ripe for cutting.

She might have had a different life.
The child was born on a cabin floor.

That cabin has always been there,
and the split light combs the shortleaf pine.

I am glad of the hate
visited upon me.

It did not come from my father.
The man paces back and forth in my dream.

Each night he kills me.
Each night I allow it to happen

because I know I will wake.
I am grateful for this, for waking,

for my father and mother,
for having known mercy.

HER HAND, THE COMPASS

My neighbor walks with wide steps around the yellow crocuses,
moves her hand over the life that kicks in her.

She doesn't know that this child will never be born.
She sees that someone cut back the herbs in the garden

and can't understand it. Oregano, basil, mint.
They are all green and want to be tasted.

When the chives are cut, they come back.
With her finger, she traces a map

and the child hears its soft drum:
Here are the crocuses and peonies.

Here is where your father, whom you do not know
writes in notebooks. Here is where he will scold you,

then forgive you. Here, the lights
will only stun you a minute. You will shoot up like thyme

and tangle with the world, where everything
wants to be meant for something bigger.

LEARNING TO SPEAK

October's state fair weekend: gasoline and corn dogs, funnel cake, sweat. Big Tex, the colossal cowboy, lurched in the wind.

The stranger's hand recoiled like a clam, fingers retracting into the slippery palm.

And the words would not come, and I could not call out. Only *book* or *banana*, but never *I am lost*, never *I have lost my father*.

I sat in a room with a woman in a white coat. She asked me to name the pictures on the wall.

Peanut butter sandwich. Yellow—no, not "la," "ya." Good. *Sandbox.*

The window on the door was crosshatched with white tape. *Stripes.* Keep your tongue behind your teeth.

In Fort Worth, the creek that ran behind our house was sludge. When Father found a dinosaur footprint, I spread my fingers out between its toes. *Prehistoric*, he said.

The day after the dentist took out his wisdom teeth, I peered into my father's room. It was dark—his mouth full of cotton.

I heard Mother say *unhappy.*

When she went out into the yard one day, I crawled beneath the sink. The words would not come. And I could not call out. *Shh*, I taught myself.

The cabinet air was damp; a drop of water ran down my back. I heard his voice and pushed on the back of the door.

He smiled slowly, running his finger along the drum of his stethoscope. *We're moving back*, he said, and she pressed her hand to his face.

Houses, fences, and cattle flashed like negatives across each window. His hand on the dial, he sang. His squelched voice: *Maybe I didn't love you, as often as I should have . . . You were always on my mind, you were always on my mind . . .*

His hand would rest on Mother's knee, and I would lean forward, check on the baby, make sure she hadn't fallen out of her car seat.

And his boot tapped beside the pedal, softly, like *chapters*, opening and closing.

PROPAGATION

At the Halloween party, I sat in the neighbor's lap.
His hand pressed against my knee. He said
we had the same birthday. He didn't wear a costume.
He spoke in a voice like mud and I looked
for my sister. We'd only lived on the block a few months,
and already I was having nightmares. I'd wake up
on the cold wood floor. Out the window,
the neighbors' house stood like a fortress. White
as the castles in books. Years later, that neighbor
would open his wife's throat with a pair of scissors.
In the daytime, my sister and I sat in the yard
and dug up our father's onions. I would tell her
of the two girls in the castle, and their mother
and father, as I handed her a moon-faced bulb.
We peered over the fence and bit.

THE MUSE, POSING AS MARIA

. . . the sculpture represented Maria Mitchell's
"singularly sweet and blameless life."
                    —On Saint-Gaudens's "The Angel of Purity"

But there is always more to it.
The muse, the sculptor's mistress: her stone-kept pout,
plummet of the neck, the yawning eyes.
And Maria. Dead, diphtheria, age twenty-two,
never married. The muse, his whore, but alive
in a body not made of stone. And the stone, too,
carried up from the quarry, and what he cut away.

The two of us stand before the sculpture
a century after. You turn and say,
You're not who I thought you were.
What about before, I say, *when it was different?*
You say, *She is beautiful.*
I say, *Why,* thinking her hooded eyes, the palms'
flesh like white plums, the ruched wings.
She just is.

Outside, the wind is strong enough
to carve ice. Outside, the girl I once was
shoulders the cold.

THE UNCOMMON MIRROR

Twin, turn away from the fire
and look down at the clouds.

I carry you as a woman's
full water gourd

or the crest of green and gold feathers
that weighs on a pheasant's crown.

Turn away from the onlookers.
Think only of what is worth seeing:

our mother as she pestles
coriander in a wooden bowl,

the black monsoon clouds
clutching the river,

the mongoose circling the cobra
as the sun rounds your neck.

Do not think of the chapel
across the river

or the doctors'
upended faces

that rise up in horror.
Breathe in the clotted air.

Do not remember the midwife
who, in terror, threw

us into the fire. Do not
think of the blue

and red of the flames
or the white of the midwife's dress.

Think of India. Think of Kolkata.
Think of the painful

beauty of the crescent moon.
And when there is too much,

let fall the river
down both our faces.

SOUND OF THE SPINNING WHEEL

The devil has told you that! The devil has told you that!
—The Brothers Grimm, "Rumpelstiltskin"

At night, in that threadbare space
where the cry of a child should be,

a little man with hammered gems for teeth
whispers his lines in my ear.

He riddles my heart. Turns
the rest of me to cheesecloth.

Around my throat he spins a red scarf
because I cannot say what cannot be said,

and I wear that scarf against the wind
that blows through me.

Born out of loneliness,
he comes only with death:

the smell of a child's bloomy breath
and the earth crushed under the weight of a body.

So I become someone else,
my head full of tinnitus and fruit,

pitted and undiscerning.
I put my ears to the ground

until they are planted there
and I begin to hear the ground's singing,

the dead and their thousand
dying verses. Only then can I say

what I could not say, that there is a hole in me
where a worm crawled through.

That hole says *mother*.
It says *father*. It says *mother, father*

until I rise from my barrenness,
and tear myself in two.

THE PHEASANT

. . . the variety of monsters will be found to be infinite.
—John Hunter, 1780

1

For eleven springs against the April snow, the spots on her feathers
were black eyes, the thin reeds of grass lashes, and she hunched

and cooed as the bright male beat his wings against her,
bobbed his necklaced neck like a ship's gilded bow,

held her head with his beak and curled his tail feathers
around her body. The pheasant came to the woman

each morning for food and each year presented her
with a small brood of chicks. The woman began to see

herself in the bird: the way she pecked and rounded up
her young; her subtle beauty, dulled like tinted paint;

the way she curtsied before the glamorous male,
who, almost refined, tucked her beneath him.

2

This year, after molting, the pheasant is no longer egg-colored
but deep golden red, her long truss of feathers

low to the ground on her small frame. Her spots
not eyes but sapphires, and the long cleft of her tail

cleaves the sky into two skies. The woman
calls in the scientists and they pin down the bird with gloved hands.

They prod beneath the spectral plumage. They pluck
and hypothesize and write things down in notebooks.

The colors of her are fire, imperious against the pale
wood table, the humbled white of the snow.

OYSTER

When you came back from Westhampton,
you brought a handful of shells.
One, an oyster, was splintered and coarse in places,
and in others, layered with dark silt.
There was a hole in the palm of it, where life
must have been.
                    I know a shell can't feel
but wonder anyway:
the absence of muscle, that spot, its belly,
like that spot in me you left. It's funny. It seems for months
I've been waiting.
Everything is just how you left it. If you look closely,
there is a ring, mother-of-pearl, around the hole.
It's the place closest to pain that shines.

INVOCATION

Praise my coronary artery, the Red River, and passing it,
  through the country
of my heart, the Vena Cava, which is the Rio Grande.

Praise the piñon pine, steel-toed boots, what looking out
stirs inside: patches of wildflower that streak the Texas highway,

Enchanted Rock and the Brazos, God's river-arms; praise
its prison songs that sing low like grandfathers—

my spleen, gallbladder and stomach, immigrant hills
my great-grandparents crossed; my capillaries, the feathers

Oma wore in her hair. Praise the whitetail fawn we found, dead
a day, its neck caught between barbs, and praise

my father's stethoscope that always hears what beats.
Praise the Great Plains, the geode caves, arrowheads carved from bone.

Praise my bronchial pathways, breathing their thousand branches,
the bluebonnet, and Baby Blue, the old Ford pickup. Praise this land,

its two hills, the house my parents planned to build.
What the flood will take from us and what will remain.

Praise the elk heads on basement walls: those lords, specters
of my family, cast like daguerreotypes in each marble eye.

∞

MATRYOSHKA

1

When you take away the children
the mother is empty. Her round head
shrouded in red, her lips thick
and pursed, her cheeks rouged
with big circles of flush. And her eyes—
she is keeping her inside secret.
The matryoshka's arms, creased
with plumpness, hug
a glossed rose. Sprigs
of cornflower and baby's breath.
If you look closer, a thin line
cuts the rose. This is where
the mother is broken.

2

I have discovered the mother
inside the mother. Her eyes
are dark like mine. She doesn't want
what is inside her. Her arms:
thin. Her collar: drab.
Her lashes: straight.
Her flower is not a rose. This mother
fits better in my hand. When I pull
her open, she creaks.

3

The last mother has no arms,
no dress, no collar.
But she is smiling.
She breaks willingly.
I twist her open
and find myself. Each mother
becomes my daughter and I become
each mother. I hold myself
in my hand. This is my secret—
I have seen how small
I can be. I will put
the wooden child back inside me.
And the woman inside me. And the woman
inside me. And the woman inside me.

PLAYING TORNADO

The Great Mouth flicks its tongue
and drinks from me: rootlet,
fingers half-hearted in the plain's dirt.
This is how I wanted to go,
winded, struck and drunk by sky. I am a staff
and the cattle are sea, a water-wall of black and white,
galloping V. But this never really happens.

A furious beauty, my teacher says, looking through
the skylight that doesn't break.
The Great Mouth says I'm clairvoyant.
It's what I want to hear. He says I'll sing,
but I am no singer. Remember our game?

The haul of towels and dolls and Easter baskets
scattered across the lawn like limbs.
My sister's arms were propellers, her mouth
a fledgling's, drinking from the storm's open wormhole.

She received the greening sky as the needled face
of a prickly pear. I stayed inside. I was jinxed:
I'd seen a ghost, a girl on the merry-go-round;
I was sure she'd seen me. Sure some god
would dip his spoon of wind into the living room.
Sure he would take my body and make it his.

Take it, I thought. Take me, when I watched my sister cross
the street. And later, on the tree swing, when
the branch creaked, groaned, and in the split-second
before it fell, I saved only myself. I hate
this memory, the wind had come shouting from her lungs,

her asking eyes. Later, I wrote my wish
and slipped the paper in the rubber neck of a green balloon.
That wish to open the heart's airy cavern: no more
to lose. I held my broken promise in my hands and blew.

CIVILIZATION

We were mammoths then.
Our tusks jutted
into the star-soaked nights.
There was plenty
of tall, lush grass.
At night, alone, we would grieve.
There were so many burdens,
and we wanted them gone.
One day it came,
the flood. At the end,
you tried to lift me
from the water.
Later, like now,
you made music so pure
it would kill. Each note
was like a graveyard
or unbearable light. Even I
could not resist
turning over my shoulder.
We descend into worlds
so large, only to find
they are just under our feet.
Later, and much later now,
we walk through a park.
We run our hands
along the rocks
in the creek bed.
We stand on a bridge.
Standing on the bridge,
we look at our own bones.

My bones lie across yours.
You lift me,
as you are always lifting,
as I am always suspended.

MY NAME IN SLEEP

The night of the half-moon, a pack of wolves
    scratched down the back door,
and I could not stop them. I didn't want to.
    Call yourself coyote. Call me white horse.
This means nothing of freedom. It means we want
    to name the thing between us.
The Lakotas dreamed the West into birds whose wings
    were blackest thunder,
whose eyes blazed lightning. It has rained for days
    and this morning we knelt in the yard together
to feel the softness of the grass. Your boy is sick.
    The doctors cannot find what's wrong.
You lean on my shoulder, not
    crying. I am not a mother. But look at the moon tonight
blinking through clouds that cover its half-face
    as hands. I give myself
to the wolves. I will be a part of the wolves,
    I will be part-wolf, the wolves continue in my dream;
I will be a horse, a woman, never
    a mother, though you or I may dream it.
I hear you speaking to your son in sleep. When he is well, I will start
    to admit it is my name I want to hear.
You say you try to lift your thoughts through and above
    the clouds to watch them disappear.
The moon is a bowl of night birds. Kneeling by the bed,
    hands cupped in a prayer he has not yet learned,
is him, your boy, and in his eyes, lightning.

VOYAGER

Ann Druyan, hooked to electrodes for an EEG that
will be launched with the spacecraft Voyager,
thinks of her future husband, Carl Sagan

1

On the shore, I cup my hands
around my mouth, ocean churning at my feet,

to ask the three white ships
in the distance how to love.

The waves bare their foamy teeth.
The louder I call, the further

the ships wane on the horizon's flat map.
I disappear inside the mouth.

Whale-call of night, the sea's dark,
each briny word an oyster on my tongue.

How many loves can live inside the body?
Who will I have to cast out?

2

With the golden record, we pitched
life on earth into the solar system: Hello

in 55 languages (the most beautiful, in Arabic:
Greetings to our friends in the stars, may time bring us together),

the sounds of thunder, of waves,
chickadees, dolphins. Tibetan bowls,

Blind Willie Johnson in his salt-covered voice, singing,
Dark was the night, cold was the ground,

a Navajo chant, a Peruvian wedding song,
the image of a nursing mother,

diagram of internal organs, photographs
of a mountain climber, an old man with dog and flowers.

3

I think of Ann, her forehead wreathed
in electrode cups—

one woman's heart
reeling, at 35,000 miles an hour

on the great open sea
of interstellar space.

You tilt your wine in the air, say
there is a place for us,

but not in this world.
With every lift of the glass,

I hear my own heart
a galaxy away, propelling

down that black ocean,
both of the earth and outside it,

both mine and not mine,
its language impossible to speak.

THE OUTER CORE

I am sitting with the moon and we are drinking from the sky.
We break open the earth like an egg and look inside.
We discover equinox, sulfur, Aurora Borealis.
I try and explain the names for things, why "westward"
is different from "drift." We find the dead
beneath the rheumy crystals of quartz.
The moon pulls the ocean to a curl and settles down,
fat and orange, beside me. We discover
each molecule, passing through and out of me,
that has already known many others. Because there is no
center, the moon keeps saying, we must give ourselves away.

FOURTH STATE OF MATTER

The day Big Tex burned, it began in the throat—
        an utterance that caught fire.
That day, the other fathers

        gorged lazily on turkey legs,
graying beards littered with pink meat.
        I knew to find Big Tex, whose 75-gallon hat

mooned over the crowd, giant steel arm
        lurching up and down like an oil derrick.
I tracked his cowboy drawl to the fairground's center,

        scanned the dune of faces for my father's
thick glasses and cumulous blond hair.
        Now, the photograph of that day (my father and I,

his blue t-shirt, my mustard-drenched corn dog)
        is an envoy for the memory—
I remember myself then

        only through the mediation of film: nebula
of my child life strewn across the far reaches of some sky.
        Later, I saw that my father's life wasn't whole

but scattered, and didn't really belong to me;
        as he unraveled in grief for his own parents,
I didn't relate, but suddenly, I could imagine

        the absolute zero of loss—I wanted, too, to be done
with being one person, the pixels of a single moment
        converging, bursting into flame.

TIPI

Tipi and I were the same age. His eyes, whitish and filmy,
tracked me vaguely when I opened and closed

the stable door, fed him an apple from my hand.
Over one hill then another we rode, until I couldn't hear

the voices at the barn or my brother chipping geodes
with a hammer, the purple smack of agate.

Tipi and I were alone in the hills
and we were so quiet. The longhorns grazed

beside the pond and deer peered around the bur oaks
and the redbuds. When I fell, it was as if I were suspended,

reins slipping through my hands like a lost argument;
Tipi bucked, the russet ring around his eye like a bruise.

Not then, but eventually, both our lives
would end, no matter the gall, the drive,

how much we fought. Tipi wandered back
to the barn and I, picking burrs from my arms and legs,

looking across to the other hill spattered with Indian paintbrush,
knew it was me who had fallen, and not the horse that threw me.

AFTER TWENTY JUNES

Today's mild heat rewinds the mind's clock
twenty years: at our old house, I climb

the magnolia (blossoms open as new minds),
take my box from a nook in wood, and whisper myself

into a trance: tiger's eye, fool's gold, amethyst, geode,
serpentine, bloodstone, moonstone, agate.

I identify, catalogue. I do not know
that later I will do this with my heart.

I glitter-glue my weird secrets into bark.
When the phone rings, it's the boy

who's now gone. He wants to play army.
He is the expanse of my blackening sky.

I do not know yet that I will feel
his phantom hand when I'm drunk at the funeral.

The plywood cries a pulpy wax
into the bark. Dad takes down

the rotted planks one by one.
The grass grows and is cut and grows again

and the wind picks up and I'm turning
to knock on the door of that house

but I don't live there anymore. The man beside me
is a shadowy figure of child-dreams.

The earth dreams up the sky.
The moon is an opal, the stars

emeralds. I walk out. I look up.
The great mother looks back, flashes

her comet-tail smile. I am pregnant
with the spangled stone of time.

HYPOTHESIS

If we climb the jet bridge
in our wool socks.
If my brother is last
so we don't see him fall.
If he falls beneath a holly bush,
his blond hair a sleeping
animal against the eyes,
opal skin like a jeweler's light.
If no time has passed.
If the planes overhead
make shadows on his face.
If I dream this every night
for years. If the light,
its tilting mirror, strikes the skin
and I see these many years
have passed. If it is my face.
I, a child in this world.
If my brother wears his funeral suit,
my sister in green like a garden,
my father's eyes to the ground
and mine looking up.
This, then, our strange procession,
climbing the bridge,
boarding the plane,
our winged eclipse,
our momentary shadow.

OFFERING

Over the fog-dipped trees, a flock
of whooping cranes, led by an ultralight aircraft.

The sun on nylon wings is almost like warmth
on feathers; the pilot, a woman dressed as a bird,

squints through mesh eyes, careful of the V
that unevenly heaves around her.

Weeks ago, the refugees brooded: rigged wings
of a taxidermied mother—swan-bodied,

head of a whooping crane.
A man with a puppeted hand

taught them how to eat and drink.
Now, with the fall migration, new inventions

of color: white wings, black-tipped,
spilled ink on new paper,

and the cranes' heads, ignited
by a torrent of red, camouflaged

against the blaze of autumn maple.
Scientists discover later

the cranes abandoning their eggs,
not knowing their own biology,

that cranes are cranes; humans, human.
Each October, though, the Wisconsin sky is swollen

with sound: whoops of the young cranes,
wings like laundry in wind;

the avian aircraft, a washboard
clacking over the horizon.

NIAGARA

The cliffs are studded fists. We cross over
to the Canadian side, to Horseshoe Falls.
Where the water tumbles,
there is a space of quiet—

Geese fly in from three directions to make a skein.
You speak of your grandfather in a low voice,
the one who survived the war. The sun
catches the place on your eye where a cataract
was removed. A boat chortles as it pulls
away from the pier and disappears into the spray.

Nothing survives where the water strikes
the rocks, an unremitting smack,
a motor-like drone. To think
of coming across it for the first time.
To think, how many years
we've been vanishing,
as the water against the boat's hull.
To think, your eyes—
how they gather up the river like a skirt.

NARRATIVE

Because there is no principle of love,
you and I ride horses to a curve in the lake.
Because we are ever-expanding cosmic bodies,
but do not understand physics,
my horse will be named Dakota, and yours
Chip, and when he bends his head to drink,
the forces of memory and dark energy
erupt from the water like cattails. When we say love,
we only know how for a few moments.
And keep insisting on different versions
of the same story. Chaos or, better,
the original emptiness is always a constant.
One horse bellows, and the other answers
with a clip of her shoe
on a nearby stone. Because suffering
is difficult to define, the lake is this blue
only once. The horses toss the reins from their necks.
They have been here a long time,
and know only the old ways.
When we return home, we keep trying different ways
to feel the same. And the old sun sets on the stables.
The stable man lies down beside his wife.
They hear hooves that kick against stable doors.
She cannot sleep without that sound.

STORM COMING

Before rain, my father stands on the porch,
drawing in the metallic air. In his face,

I look for my own. I've seen the way he is
with his father. He counts down the lightning.

The sky swells like an oath.
Dad, he'll say, *how about next time*

we'll go and get some of those peaches you like,
out by the highway? He'll laugh a laugh

that knows its own ending. And the drops fall,
just like he promised. The storm is birth and death

in only minutes. So we laugh, knowing
we don't have the time to love it.

Notes

"Echolocation": "When my life was ebbing away, I remembered you, Lord, and my prayer rose to you, to your holy temple." This is from the Bible, in Jonah 2:7.

"Chrysalis": The poem was inspired by the butterfly rainforest webcam, which streams from the Florida Museum of Natural History. The anecdote about Cosimo de Medici visiting Jan Swammerdam's curiosity cabinet is taken from *Renaissance and Revolution: Humanists, Scholars, Craftsmen and Natural Philosophers in Early Modern Europe*, edited by J. V. Field and Frank A. J. L. James (Cambridge University Press, 1997).

"Nocturne for the Elephant": See the account of a piano tuner and an elephant in "On the Difference of Structure between the Human Membrana Tympani and That of the Elephant" by Everard Home, *Philosophical Transactions of the Royal Society of London*, Volume 113 (1823).

"House of Making": An imagined conversation between myself and my mentor Bruce Bond, this poem is part of a larger collaborative work called "Listening as Dialogue." For further reading on the sounds of a dead yeast cell, see the National Public Radio feature story "Researchers Listen to Yeast Cells."

"Superficial Heart": This poem was inspired by "A Description of a Very Unusual Formation of the Human Heart" by James Wilson and Matthew Baillie, in *Philosophical Transactions of the Royal Society*, Volume 88 (1798).

"The Dream, the Sleeping Gypsy": This poem's title derives from the titles of two Henri Rousseau paintings.

"Our Lady of the Rio Grande": This poem was inspired by a large-scale installation work by Dan Flavin, "untitled (Marfa project), 1996," which is at the Chinati Foundation in Marfa, Texas.

"The Muse, Posing as Maria": Augustus Saint-Gaudens's *The Angel of Purity*, now in the Philadelphia Museum of Art, was commissioned by the parents of Maria Gouverneur Mitchell on the occasion of her untimely death in 1898. The features of the angel are believed to have been modeled on those of the sculptor's mistress.

"The Uncommon Mirror": "When the child cried, the features of the superior head were not always affected; and, when the child smiled, the features of the superior head did not sympathize in that action." —Everard Home, on a child born with a double head, *Philosophical Transactions of the Royal Society of London*, Volume 100 (1810).

"The Pheasant": The epigraph for this poem is taken from John Hunter's "An Account of an Extraordinary Pheasant" in *Philosophical Transactions of the Royal Society of London*, Volume 70 (1780).

"Civilization": This poem is born out of the archaeological discoveries at the Waco Mammoth National Monument in Waco, Texas.

"My Name in Sleep": "When a vision comes from the thunder beings of the west, it comes with terror like a thunder storm; but when the storm of vision has passed, the world is greener and happier; for wherever the truth of vision comes upon the world, it is like a rain. The world, you see, is happier after the terror of the storm." This is from *Black Elk Speaks* by Nicholas Black Elk, as told to John G. Neihardt, originally published in 1932 and available in various editions.

"*Voyager*": Ann Druyan's EEG revery occurred in 1977, according to an interview with her featured on the radio show and podcast Radiolab in an episode entitled "Space" (Season 2, Episode 5).

"Fourth State of Matter": This poem refers to an event reported as "Electrical Fire Destroys Big Tex, State Fair's Folksy Icon Since 1952," in *The Dallas Morning News* (October 19, 2012).

"Offering": This poem was inspired by "Raising Crane," a short Radiolab podcast (December 3, 2012).

"Narrative": "Chaos or, better, / the original emptiness" refers to a sense that the stable element in abusive relationships is the idea that the world isn't stable, thus love cannot be.

Acknowledgments

Many thanks to the editors of the following publications where these poems first appeared, sometimes in slightly different versions.

The Adroit Journal: "Echolocation"

All We Can Hold: A Collection of Poetry on Motherhood (online anthology): "Her Hand, the Compass"

Blueshift Journal: "Playing Tornado"

The Boiler Journal: "Mirror, "Our Lady of the Rio Grande," and "Phosphene"

Copper Nickel: "Necrosis"

I–70 Review: "Bathsheba as Poet" and "Invocation"

Louisville Review: "Pomegranate"

Mississippi Review: "Civilization"

The Missouri Review: "Chrysalis," "Fourth State of Matter," "Sound of the Spinning Wheel," and "Storm Coming"

Mudlark: "Nocturne for the Elephant," "The Dream, the Sleeping Gypsy," "The Muse, Posing as Maria," and "The Pheasant"

The New Guard: "Matryoshka"

North American Review: "Marvels of the Invisible"

Oberon Poetry Journal: "My Name in Sleep"

Poetry International: "The Dream, the Sleeping Gypsy" (reprint)

The Rattling Wall: "I Am not Thine, but Thee," "Superficial Heart," and "Tipi"

Smartish Pace: "Niagara"

Thir d Coast: "Narrative"

"Echolocation" also appeared in the 2016 *Orison Anthology,* and "Marvels of the Invisible" also appeared in *Best New Poets 2014.* "Narrative" was chosen for the 2013 *Third Coast* Poetry Prize and was featured on the Verse Daily website. "Storm Coming" was featured as the Poem of the Week at *The Missouri Review.*

With the deepest gratitude, I thank my teachers for their unwavering support and generosity, and for believing in these poems: Bruce Bond, Kyle Dargan, Pete Fairchild, David Keplinger, and Corey Marks. Thank you, Jeffrey Harrison, for believing in this book, and many thanks to Tupelo Press for your kindness and support.

I am eternally grateful for my family's love: Mom, Dad, Susu, Pop, Jamey, and Hayden. And to my Opa, who inspired many of these poems. To my friends, my other family, thank you for everything you've taught me and for reading these poems again and again—especially Caitlin Pryor and Maia Gil'Adi. Thank you to my students, who teach me more about the world every day.

Other Books from Tupelo Press

See our complete list at www.tupelopress.org